This B
Belongs To

Made in United States
Troutdale, OR
05/20/2024

19841012R00056